CLARITY IS POWER

“Clarity is Power" book series, is a collection of wisdom from thought-provoking Q and A with renowned Mahatria. His unique gift of answering questions spontaneously is captured in this book, offering life-changing insights.

The "Clarity is Power" series comprises 11 illuminating volumes, each addressing essential aspects of life:

1. Attitudes
2. Self-Discipline
3. Emotional Development
4. Relationships
5. Marriage
6. Parenting
7. Student Life
8. Career Growth
9. Leadership and Entrepreneurship
10. Spirituality
11. Faith

Mahatria Spiritualist | Thought leader | Diviner of infinitheism

For nearly three decades, Mahatria has empowered millions worldwide to achieve holistic abundance. His profound wisdom uplifts people in health, wealth, love, bliss, and spirituality.

infinitheism, the path divined by Mahatria, inspires breakthroughs for anyone who ardently desires abundance by transforming the human spirit to have faith in its infinite potential.

First published in India

Manjul Publishing House

• 2nd Floor, Usha Preet Complex,
42 Malviya Nagar, Bhopal 462 003 - India
• C-16, Sector 3, Noida, Uttar Pradesh 201301 – India
Website: www.manjulindia.com

Distribution Centres:
Ahmedabad, Bengaluru, Bhopal, Kolkata, Chennai,
Hyderabad, Mumbai, New Delhi, Pune

In association with:

infinitheism

3, 3rd Cross Road, R A Puram,
Chennai, Tamil Nadu, India
www.infinitheism.com

MARRIAGE (CLARITY IS POWER)

by

This edition first published in 2016
Third impression 2024

ISBN 978-93-5543-432-6

Printed and bound in India by Thomson Press (India) Ltd.

MARRIAGE

mahātria

CONTENTS

1	A marriage proposal has come for me from a highly reputed family. But they say that I should not work after marriage. I am a B.E. in Computer Science and am doing very well in my career. I am confused.	6
2	How important are looks for a good marriage?	10
3	My mother-in-law is not very clean, but I like my house to be spotless. I am working, so I don't find much time to clean the house. Sometimes I feel we have to move out, but that's not a good solution. Please suggest a solution.	14
4	I will soon be getting married; it's an arranged marriage and both of us are happy with this decision. What's your advice for an exemplary married life?	18
5	My wife and I quarrel every day. The issue is always small. We both lose our control. Our life is colourless. Divorce isn't the solution. Should one of us end our life?	22
6	My profession demands working late nights and on Sundays. I have found my soul mate. His standpoint is, "Unless you get your work-life right, we can't get married." I cannot lose either. I need help.	26
7	Is it really possible to love my wife the way I loved her on the first day till the last day of her or my life? We have been married for five years and our relationship has become dry. Please guide me.	30
8	My 32-year-old sister is very passionate about her career. Few marriage proposals had come but nothing has transpired. Now she thinks that most marriages fail, and ambitious girls quit their career after marriage. So, she does not want to get married. What should I do as a brother?	34

CONTENTS

9	My husband has time for cricket, TV, friends, club activities, etc. beyond his normal office work. But whenever I ask for outing with him, he puts on a 'Busy' tag. This irritates me beyond words. How do I deal with this? (Basically, he is a nice guy!)	**38**
10	My husband and I are honest to our emotions, and there are times when discussions turn into fights and of course later we patch up. I am concerned now because, of late, this fight between us is affecting our children. What should we do?	**42**
11	I have been married for three years and I have a girl child. Our parents did not match our horoscope. My husband forgets his duties and is blind towards his parents. What should I do to bring him out of the clutches of his father?	**46**
12	My alliance is not getting fixed due to too many expectations from the girls. What should I do?	**50**
13	My life has been built on the foundations of devotion to God. A marriage proposal has come from a person, who is a great social contributor, but an atheist. Should I go ahead with the proposal?	**54**
14	My husband does not want to make it big in life, but I believe in a life of abundance. I feel that if I become more successful than him, it will cause a strain in our relationship. How best can I sort this out?	**58**
15	Is having sexual feelings towards my soulmate, whom I love and respect, and expressing them explicitly wrong? I am a religious person, and I am confused about this.	**62**

1

A marriage proposal has come for me from a highly reputed family. But they say that I should not work after marriage. I am a B.E. in Computer Science and am doing very well in my career. I am confused.

Confusion comes when there is no clarity. There can be no clarity where there is no conviction. Chances are that a boy or a girl committed suicide a few years ago because they couldn't get a seat in B.E. Computer Science. Chances are that you sat in that seat and did your engineering. Now, you are not only accountable to your own education but also to that kid who ended his or her life. Where is the conviction? Why did you do your engineering? Just to keep yourself occupied for 4 years, or was it to satisfy your parent's ego, or was it out of herd mentality, or was it to just improve your horoscope value? Why a B.E. to lock yourself within the four walls? No doubt, your education will certainly help you in the future in parenting your children with their studies and also make you more socially presentable in your husband's world - but what's the point?

Marriage, in its true sense, should magnify the life of both involved. Unfortunately, more often than not, marriage becomes the end of many possibilities for women, especially in our culture. It's like this - she has already climbed a few rungs in a ladder and after marriage, she's to shift to another ladder and start from the first rung, all over again. Why?

Don't you think you are letting your potential down? Don't you think you are trading the possibilities of your life, just for the sake of a well-educated, well-placed man from a reputed family? Don't you have even this belief that in this ocean of humanity there is a man for you who will not expect you to live a lesser life in exchange for marriage? Why scream about male exploitation, if you don't have the conviction to stand up for a life worthy of your potential?

Wake up. Marriage need not be the end of an individual. Marriage can be and should be a continuity of life, of magnifying possibilities. If even you don't stand up for yourself, no one else will.

There is a wrong notion that a woman need not earn and that a man can take care of her. We don't work to earn - earning is a by-product. We work to give expression to our inner talent. We work to challenge our potential. We work to remain mentally and intellectually agile. Most importantly, we work because running a family, in this new world, is no more a full-time occupation. There is a lot of time at our disposal; let it be invested in creative pursuits - work is an avenue for it.

Never be resigned to a life where you may feel that you've betrayed your own possibilities. Stand up for yourself. This is your fight. ●

Marriage need not be
the end of an individual.
Marriage can be and should be
a continuity of life,
of magnifying possibilities.

2

How important are looks for a good marriage?

I am sure you know the answer. All of us know the answer, don't we! Surveys show that 56% of women and 43% of men are not satisfied with their looks. They have a complex about their looks. So I can understand your concern.

A lot of factors like family background, educational qualifications, geographical compatibility, financial status, religion, habits, the past of the individual and of course looks, play a very significant role in making a decision on who should be your life partner. However, none of these factors play any role in the success of a marriage. A good marriage actually begins only after all the hype of the initial years is over.

What Henry Ford stated as a management philosophy, "Coming together is a beginning. Staying together is progress. Working together is success," is much more a relationship philosophy. Preferably both, if not, at least one has to relentlessly work in the building of any relationship. Like it is with organisations, it is with lasting relationships - they have to be built.

If at all there is one factor that weighs above all other factors for the success of a marriage, for that matter the success of any relationship, it is compatibility of values.

If you want only a great beginning, then check out on the first list of factors. If you want great progress then you have no other choice than to be sure about the compatibility of values. The rest are details.

I am not saying 'looks' are nothing. I am only saying it is not everything. 'Looks' are skin deep and it is a diminishing phenomenon. 'Love' is beyond the skin and it is a growing phenomenon. And do you know that - in love, everything looks beautiful. "You look beautiful and so I love you," is transient. "I love you and so you look beautiful," is eternal. Love him and he will always look handsome to you. Love her and she will always look beautiful to you. When the heart begins to see what the eyes can never see, for the first time you will actually know what beauty is. True beauty is not seen. It is felt. ●

If at all there is one factor
that weighs above all other factors
for the success of a marriage,
for that matter
the success of any relationship,
it is compatibility of values.

3

My mother-in-law is not very clean, but I like my house to be spotless. I am working, so I don't find much time to clean the house. Sometimes I feel we have to move out, but that's not a good solution. Please suggest a solution.

Cleanliness is an attitude. Attitudes like cleanliness and personal hygiene be better cultivated in children, for, they can seldom be instilled in an adult, who has never had an inclination for cleanliness. You will be considered too fussy and finicky for raising cleanliness as an issue.

The typical phrase you will hear: "Don't blow such small issues out of proportions." So, first-of-all give-up this desire that your mother-in-law's attitude towards cleanliness can be changed. You cannot expect oranges from a mango tree and then feel frustrated with the mango tree that it is not giving you oranges. This is your mother-in-law and this is how she will continue to be.

More importantly, I wish to ask you, "Are there any flawless individual? Are you flawless?" (Make an honest whisper unto yourself.) People come as integrated packages, with their pluses and their minuses.

'Not being clean' is your mother-in-law's minus. But I am sure she has more and enough pluses to compensate for this one minus or other minuses. I tell every man and woman, if you consider your spouse to be a blessing in your life, then your primary gratitude should go to your father-in-law and mother-in-law. After all, this blessing in your life is their rearing.

Gratitude enables acceptance and tolerance of those you are grateful to. I also believe, because you are a working woman, your mother-in-law must be doing a lot of household chores to keep the house functioning. For all that, all that is required from your end is a little tolerance - extend it and be peaceful.

Moreover, if you move out, you will obviously have to get a servant to do your housekeeping. Why don't you do that now? Anyway, let's not leave a single stone unturned. Meanwhile, maintain your personal room in such a spick-and-span way that - who knows, one day she too might get inspired.

Finally, my standard reply: Put your peace above everything else. Nothing and nobody in life is worth it, if it only comes at the cost of disturbing your peace. You say cleanliness is next to godliness. I say that godliness itself is possible only through peacefulness.

Let us have a clean attitude to life before we expect the world to have the attitude to be clean. And that clean attitude I am referring to is: 'Peace is above everything else'. ●

I wish to ask you,
"Are there any
flawless individual?
Are you flawless?"

People come as
integrated packages,
with their pluses
and their minuses.

4

I will soon be getting married; it's an arranged marriage and both of us are happy with this decision. What's your advice for an exemplary married life?

Relationships are like seeds. They have to be nurtured and developed, more so in a marriage. There are a few guiding principles to a lasting relationship.

1. Over centuries of conditioning, the terms husband and wife have derived a very narrow connotation. It shrinks the scope of this relationship. Drop the words husband and wife from your very vocabulary and resolve to be 'friends for a lifetime'. Then, both the man and the woman will sometimes play the mother, sometimes the father, sometimes a cranky kid, then the mentor, the teacher, the mirror... and of course, sometimes husband and wife too.

2. From the very beginning, relate to the person and not just the body. Observe each other's thinking, discuss personal values, standpoints and convictions; get sensitised to each other's feelings, develop emotional compatibility and take time to sit together in quietude to develop a spiritual connectivity. This will bring a lot of dignity to this relationship.

3. Most spouses fall all over each other, overdo everything within the first few months and then there is no life left in that relationship. They co-exist in a dead relationship. Take it slow and make it long. Remember, less will make it more and more will make it less.

4. The past is irrelevant. The present forms the building blocks. The future is very significant, for that is where the two of you will travel together. Discussing day-to-day trifles alone, will make you fall in love. Talk future, talk dreams, talk ambitions, and resolve to play a part in each other's growth in a very objective and non-intrusive manner.

5. There is this utopian concept that after the wedding, both lives superimpose and there is only one life to live from then on. No wonder most women were forced to live as a shadow of their man in the name of marriage - they tagged on, but as frustrated, self-pitying, sacrificial individuals who felt exploited. The fact is - much after your life and my life has become our life, there is still my life and your life. 'Our' life is that intersecting space called marriage. Happiness in marriage depends on how both of you relate in 'our' space and how this space keeps growing with every passing year. However, he will continue to have his life and she should continue to have her life. This will ensure that you respect each other's space, each other's individual likes, dislikes and priorities, and most importantly, this alone will ensure that you do not suffocate each other in the name of love.

Building a great marriage is an art; so get artistic. ●

Relationships are like seeds.
They have to be
nurtured and developed,
more so in a marriage.

5

My wife and I quarrel every day. The issue is always small. We both lose our control. Our life is colourless. Divorce isn't the solution. Should one of us end our life?

First and foremost, promise me as you read this sentence, you have dropped your thoughts of suicide. Removing the head is not the solution for headache. If people with problems have to run away from life, then no one will be left. For anything, death isn't a solution. Life is.

Existence, on purpose had designed man different from woman, leaving both a little incomplete so that in embracing each other you feel that completeness. Most marriages suffer because we haven't learnt to deal with differences positively.

The basis of man is thinking and for a woman it is feeling. Don't tell a man, "Silly idea." Never tell a woman, "Silly feelings." "You did well" is a compliment to man. To a woman, "I am feeling good about what you did" is a compliment. Men act as if they can, even when they can't. Women act as if they can't, even when they can. Men are never at ease accepting their weaknesses. Women are never at ease accepting their strengths. Because man experiences love through the doors of the body, he wants his woman to be fresh and attractive. Because woman experience the body through the doors of love, she wants her man to be sensitive and caring. So, men need sweet-touchings, and women need sweet-nothings.

Man represents the sperm and hence is result-oriented. So he speaks of competition; always says, 'come to the point'; selfishly puts himself first; likes to argue; believes good fences make good neighbours. He prefers to be left alone in his psychological and physical space. On the contrary, woman represents the ovum (nurturing) and hence is process-oriented. So she speaks of cooperation; always says, 'get into the details'; selflessly puts others first; likes to share; believes good chats make good neighbours. She wants company and shares her psychological and physical space.

And above all, man can never handle the unhappiness of his woman. The only way he knows to handle her unhappiness is to escape the situation. His best comes out only when he knows his woman is happy in life. On the other hand, a woman, however successful and independent she may be, needs protective love from her man. She needs a parental touch from her man. Her best comes out only when she feels secure in her man's presence.

View the differences positively, instead of accepting yourself as you are and trying to change her - change yourself and accept her as she is; do not do to her what you do not want her to do to you, do to her what you want her to do to you. And most importantly, believe in the power of your love for her. What is not possible for love? If love cannot, nothing else can... and love alone is our salvation. I love you. ●

6

My profession demands working late nights and on Sundays. I have found my soulmate. His standpoint is, "Unless you get your work-life right, we can't get married." I cannot lose either. I need help.

Not everybody is a Mother Teresa. She lived to serve, and there was nothing more to her life. Not everybody is a Swami Vivekananda. He lived to lift humanity spiritually, and there was nothing more to his life. Not everybody is a Ramana Maharishi. He lived for and with his silence, and including his seekers - everything else was mere details in his life. They represented a purpose and to their last breath they lived for that purpose. Their lives were not defined by the roles they played, but by the purpose they served. They did, they didn't, they read, they wrote, they spoke, they worked by themselves, they worked through their teams, they organised, they inspired, they breathed - all for the purpose they represented. Their life was one indivisible whole.

With no intention to belittle anyone, truth be told, most of us are not in that league. We are mere mortals with typical (genuine) human aspirations. Our life is defined by our roles. For us, serving a purpose is one of the roles of our life and not the only purpose of our life. True, we have our rights in every role of our life; but, let us not forget, we also have our responsibilities in each of these roles. Succeeding in one role at the cost of failing in another is a life of imbalance. Will you focus on your right biceps and forsake the biceps in the left? Won't you cause your own handicap? There is no point in being a one role wonder. A life without balance isn't a life at all. It seems to be the curse of the modern generation that so many of us attempt to succeed at the cost of balance in life.

What is the difference between a canvas of colours and a painting? One is splash of colours and the other is balancing of colours. Life is all about balance.

If you are not able to take care of your own health, if you do not have quality family time, if you are not able to nurture your relationships, if you have forsaken your talents, if you haven't drenched yourself in the rains and not witnessed a sunset and haven't gazed at the night skies, if you are not able to evolve your consciousness through spiritual seeking and practices, if you don't get to have a quiet evening holding the hands of your beloved... if everything else is lost in life because you work for an organisation that works for a social cause, then the very working methodology of the organisation is questionable. Like 'charity begins at home', for an organisation, their social cause begins with the cause of their own employees. Any organisation that succeeds at the cost of the personal lives of their employees doesn't earn my salute.

In relationships, love is not only spelled l.o.v.e but it is also spelled t.i.m.e. That in which you invest time grows, and that which you starve of your time shrinks. Without quality time there can never be quality relationships. Not just for your marriage's sake, or for the sake of the standpoint of your man, but for the sake of the sheer joy of experiencing life in its entirety, achieve balance in life.

It is plain commonsense to understand, what cannot be done in 'x' hours will not get done in 'x + y' hours either. So might as well give the 'x' hours to work and take the 'y' hours to all other aspects of your life. Of course, please ensure 'x' is greater than 'y'.

Do well in your work. Sit and talk to your organisation. Any organisation with a moral conscience will always do what is right in the interest of everybody involved. When there can be a win-win situation, why not? Help your organisation to understand and it will help all of you. Do well in your marriage too. Sit and talk to your man. Any man who respects his woman will also respect her work. "I love you but I don't love what you do," is not love at all. Respecting you means also respecting what you do. There is no need for 'this or that'. 'This and that' is possible. ●

7

Is it really possible to love my wife the way I loved her on the first day till the last day of her or my life? We have been married for five years and our relationship has become dry. Please guide me.

For the immature, prolonged usage of anything creates diminishing value. For the evolved, prolonged usage and practice of anything is the only way to make it Higher, Deeper, Beyond. So, if you are the evolved, the more and more you relate to a person, you will only find more and more reasons to love them. Thus, you grow in love. For the immature, familiarity breeds contempt. Hence, they fall in love.

To sustain the depth of a relationship, especially marriage, from the very beginning, relate to the person and not just the body. This will bring a lot of dignity to the relationship.

We live in the information age. So, the contemporary human consciousness in its very nature is intellectually curious. Without the husband and wife enjoying each other's intellectual company there will be no energy in the relationship.

Talk about your agreements. Debate the disagreements. The only way to be interesting in a relationship is by discussing what the other person is interested in. Share your doubts. Share your observations. Ask for the other's point of view. Keep your face-to-face discussions as dynamic as you keep updating your Facebook pages. You should look forward to each other's company, and intellectual companionship is one of the prime ways.

The significance of the past diminishes as the present shapes our foundation. However, it's the future that holds paramount importance, as it becomes the shared journey ahead. Embrace discussions about the future to nurture your bond. Mere conversations about daily trivialities can spark affection, yet delving into the future, sharing dreams, and committing to contribute to each other's personal development in an objective and respectful manner will foster profound growth in your love for one another.

And most importantly, to keep the relationship romantic, rely on your own intuitive ways of expressing love. Don't borrow ideas from movies. That's why it is dry. Trust your instincts. Fill your days with non-sexual touch. Romance is all about freshness. From looks to garments to environment to expressions to fragrance to tone of voice to gestures there must be freshness.

An element of surprise is the undercurrent of romance. Keep surprising yourself. Keep surprising your spouse. Bring life into your expressions and thus you will bring back life into your marriage.

Marriage: One relationship that's always under construction. So, keep it going...

The only way to be interesting in a relationship is by discussing what the other person is interested in.

mahātria

8

My 32-year-old sister is very passionate about her career. Few marriage proposals had come but nothing has transpired. Now she thinks that most marriages fail, and ambitious girls quit their career after marriage. So, she does not want to get married. What should I do as a brother?

Let me start with a lighter note. The wife was pregnant, and she is going to deliver their fourth child; the husband was reading the newspaper and suddenly he screamed to the wife, 'I know our baby is going to be a Chinese baby...' She was shocked because both of them were Indians. 'How on earth for two Indians a Chinese will be born?', the wife screamed back. The husband said, 'Statistics reveals that every fourth baby in the world is Chinese'.

Instead of saying, 'Nine out of ten marriages are not happy marriages and hence I am opting out of it', I would want your sister to look at the 'one' marriage out of ten, which has turned out to be a happy marriage and believe that hers is going to be that happy marriage. All marriages do not fail and let those happy marriages be our focus of attention.

We need to understand and be sensitive to what your sister is going through, after a few rejections of marriage proposals. The most difficult part of being a girl, is to go through this transitional phase, where she is subjected to the judgment of the groom and his family. Like a HR interview, one goes through a few rounds of interview and keeps waiting with the hope to get selected. At one point, anybody would reach that threshold of frustration and feel that 'not getting married is better than getting rejected one more time'.

She is basically saying 'instead of some man coming and rejecting me I will reject all the men' and not get married at all. Let us understand that this is a reactionary response.

For a relationship to happen, initially one judges the other. This is inevitable whether it is an arranged marriage and a love marriage. Rejection is part of the game until one finds the right partner.

Right now, what your sister needs is empathy. Sit by her side and make her feel that you understand her feelings. Empathise with her feelings. Give her the emotional strength and fill her with your love. Be a friend to her during those moments. Finally, when the right proposal clicks, all this transitional misery will be forgotten.

When you are 32 years of age, it is easy to say, 'I don't need any relationship'. But as life progresses, you need a relationship with whom you can share your emotions. Emotional loneliness is greater than any other loneliness. Be there for her now; she will understand and move forward.

For a relationship to happen, initially one judges the other. This is inevitable...

9

My husband has time for cricket, TV, friends, club activities, etc. beyond his normal office work. But whenever I ask for outing with him, he puts on a 'Busy' tag. This irritates me beyond words. How do I deal with this? (Basically, he is a nice guy!)

I understand what you are going through.

As a wife you want the undivided attention of your husband and demand his exclusive time. 'When you have time for TV, why not for me?' is your argument. The annoyed husband may switch off the TV... Too irritated to talk to you, he may avoid both and take refuge in sleep!

If the nagging becomes so much, after a point, he may even withdraw from all his social activities. But he will be coming home only to have his dinner and sleep... Home will become a lodge.

Let me explain this knot in relationship with another example:

The office boy asked for a salary advance and the accountant answered in the negative. The office boy argued over why clerical staff alone were offered a salary advance. The accountant relayed the argument to the management, and the management in turn made a policy decision to completely stop giving a salary advance.

No, it isn't wrong to ask for a salary advance, but it's certainly wrong to ask, 'Give me what you have given the other'. No, it isn't wrong to ask for your husband's time, but it's certainly wrong to ask, 'Give me the time you give to the TV'. No, it isn't wrong to ask for your spouse's time, but it's certainly wrong to ask, 'Give me the time you are giving to the society'. Why is it wrong? Because...

Ask for what you want... once, twice, thrice... umpteen times... you create the possibility of getting what you asked for. Jesus Christ said, "Ask, and it shall be given you." (Matt7:7)

Instead, when you ask for what the other has got or is getting... one, you will certainly deprive yourself of the possibility of getting what you want; and two, you may tragically create the context by which others too will be deprived of what they were getting. Let me tell you, "Ask for what the others are getting, you will be deprived of it; and perhaps, others may also be deprived of it." ●

Ask for what you want...
once, twice, thrice...
umpteen times...
you create the possibility of getting
what you asked for.

10

My husband and I are honest to our emotions, and there are times when discussions turn into fights and of course later we patch up. I am concerned now because, of late, this fight between us is affecting our children. What should we do?

A great marriage is built by honest communication, and I completely agree with you. Fights between husband and wife are not abnormal and it is part of any home environment. If there are no disagreements in a home, it only means that they are not communicating enough, or they are not vocal about their disagreements! Fighting is an integral part of any family. No two human egos can coexist under one roof without fighting and that is the reality.

So being honest in expressing your emotions is not the issue. Disrespect to each other is something that children cannot handle. Fight per se does not disturb them, but disrespectful tone and language bothers them a lot. For the child who is looking at it, it is not husband and wife being disrespectful to each other; it is 'my father is not respecting my mother' or 'my mother is not respecting my father' that jeopardises them. It is a double trauma for them. This will create insecurity in them towards any relationship that they come across in their lives.

Your son or daughter will go into a marriage scared of being disrespected or shrink whenever somebody raises their voice against them. In some cases, they might go to the other extreme and believe that putting up an emotional drama or tantrum will get them whatever they want.

No child grown in an environment where he or she did not see the father and mother respecting each other grows into an adulthood of emotional stability. As your child grows and moves into the adult world, somebody else out there have to bear the imperfections and effect of insecurity of your child and compensate for the inadequacies. Either you can work it out now in such a way that fights do not turn into disrespect, or you are making the world work a lot more in the future on your behalf. Let there not be one more problem in the world because of you. Let there be one more solution in the world through your parenting.

Along with arguments let them also hear a few appreciative words about your spouse from you. Speak about a worthy quality in your spouse with as much openness and honesty as you do when you fight. In their presence express your love for each other. These positive expressions organically build their emotional stability.

The greatest gift that parents can give their children is emotional stability. We owe it to them. ●

Let there not be one more problem in the world because of you.

Let there be one more solution in the world through your parenting.

11

I have been married for three years and I have a girl child. Our parents did not match our horoscope. My husband forgets his duties and is blind towards his parents. What should I do to bring him out of the clutches of his father?

First and foremost understand that any solution depends on focusing your attention on factors you can control, and more importantly, not wasting your attention on factors that are beyond your control. There is no point in now thinking, "Horoscopes were not matched." That's a three-year-old story. The more and more you build a story with factors that are beyond your control the less are the possibilities that you can solve them. Start thinking about factors you can control.

Secondly, by the very law of life, nothing can happen FOR you by thinking AGAINST others. You don't have to kill one relationship, in order to develop another relationship. In fact, this approach has never solved any relationship issues. The more you resist, the more it will persist. By disliking your husband's world, you only create more of a gap in your own relationship with your husband. Stop looking at his father as a villain in the story of your marriage. Start thinking as to how you can become the hero in your story.

Thirdly, by very design and innate nature, men get drawn towards a happy woman, as much as women seek the company of a man who demonstrates protective love. I can understand your daughter and you are missing the protective love of your husband. But, the more and more you transform yourself into a demonstratively, visibly, expressively happy woman, almost like a magnet, you would draw him more and more towards you.

Beyond the differences, beyond the day-to-day issues, beyond the stress of competitive life, it is imperative that men demonstrate the emotional maturity to be a source of protective love, and women display the emotional maturity to be a source of happiness. It is only in such an environment a peaceful family is experienced.

In your case, right now, your husband finds more happiness when he is with his parents than when he is with you. This is disturbing you. You dump this disturbance on him. This is driving him even further away from you. Wrong cannot fight wrong. It will only make things more wrong. You need the right approach to deal with the wrong. And, the right approach should begin with you. Transform yourself into a happy magnet. Slowly, but surely, he will become yours; of course, he will still belong to his parents too.

Finally, the cricketing genius Imran Khan once said, “Under my captaincy, we have won more matches against India because I taught my team to think, 'How can we win?' and asked them to stop thinking, 'How can we defeat them?'” My dear, focus on winning your husband into your life, and stop thinking about how to defeat your husband's parents.

Any solution depends on focusing your attention on factors you can control, and more importantly, not wasting your attention on factors that are beyond your control.

12

My alliance is not getting fixed due to too many expectations from the girls. What should I do?

Don't take this phase so seriously. See it as a game. Imagine 125 girls and 125 boys have gone on a picnic and are ready to play a game called 'Find your Pair'. Two sets of 125 cards, each carrying a different object, are distributed to the boys and girls.

Let's say you get a card that reads 'Strawberry'. One of the 125 girls is also 'Strawberry'. Now you have to find your 'one and only' Strawberry partner. "Are you my 'Strawberry'?" you ask someone at the start of the game. "No, I am 'Mango'," she replies.

Now will you both get upset and start crying? Actually, you will laugh, wish each other good luck and move on. The next one turns to be 'Apple', the one after that 'Rose' and the other 'Tomato'.

Keep playing. Somewhere in this crowd, someone is going through exactly what you are going through. Your 'Strawberry' is there somewhere in the crowd, bumping into 'Lotus', 'Pumpkin' and 'Coconut'. Keep playing. Wait for the click till the two 'Strawberries' meet.

Why should you choose an 'Apple' or a 'Blueberry' when you are a 'Strawberry'? Know that Ms. Strawberry is somewhere out there looking for you. Soon, you will find each other and together you'll be the best 'Strawberry' milkshake the world has experienced!!!

God's delays are not God's denials. Will you find your strawberry isn't the question? When will you... is the question. Your strawberry is already waiting for you somewhere... Search with faith. Search in faith. In the end, it will all be worth it. ●

Somewhere in this crowd,
someone is going through
exactly what you are going through.
Your 'Strawberry' is there
somewhere in the crowd,
bumping into
'Lotus', 'Pumpkin' and 'Coconut'.

Keep playing.
Wait for the click
till the two 'Strawberries' meet.

13

My life has been built on the foundations of devotion to God. A marriage proposal has come from a person, who is a great social contributor, but an atheist. Should I go ahead with the proposal?

Man and woman are designed wonderfully different. A great marriage is all about celebrating the differences. However, when the difference is in the value system of each other, then it shakes the very root of the relationship.

True, every human being is unique and they have the right to be different. Human beings aren't commodities. Everybody cannot be put into one basket. While sameness creates a relationship, it is the differences that liven up a relationship. Yet, when the differences are in the core values, then your entire married life will be one of negotiations and compromises.

It is not about theism or atheism - both are beliefs. It is about what matters the most to you - your devotion and your God - is a matter of joke to him. And trust me, a relationship with this difference is going to be constantly hurting. When what sentimentally matters to you is to be a matter of ridicule to the other, then there can never be emotional stability in that relationship. Matha, Pitha, Guru, Deivam... on these four factors, even if there is no collective acceptance, at least, there has to be mutual respect for a relationship to progress and succeed.

Being an atheist doesn't make him a bad person. Just that he is not the right person for you... nor would you be for him. Put compatibility of values above everything. The rest are details. ●

While sameness creates a relationship, it is the differences that liven up a relationship.

Yet, when the differences are in the core values, then your entire married life will be one of negotiations and compromises.

14

My husband does not want to make it big in life, but I believe in a life of abundance. I feel that if I become more successful than him, it will cause a strain in our relationship. How best can I sort this out?

We all have very different definitions of success. What 'big in life' means to you and what it means to your husband can be very different. What 'abundance' means to you and what it means to your husband can be very different.

Rain fills the size of the vessel. The size of your life depends on the size of your thinking. Life gives you what you believe life to be. You cannot push a man beyond the definitions he holds in his mind. You cannot change the life of a man without changing his belief systems. And some beliefs are so hard-wired that they cannot be changed from outside. Beliefs change through self-realisation and not by listening to a lectured communication.

In fact, your attempt to change your husband, very much against what he believes in, will be a very frustrating experience for him and a tiring one for you. If my inference is right, the very bone of contention between the two of you must be, how you want to define your future and how he thinks it must be. You are expecting a radically different future, compared to your present. He is only expecting a future with minimum modification to his present.

'To contribute to his growth and development' is your expression of love for him. But because his definition of love is 'to accept him as he is', it must be hurting him that you are all the time trying to change him. And by the same definition, because he must be accepting and celebrating you 'just' as you are, it must be hurting you. Your hurt is, "Why is he not participating enough in making me a success?"

My dear, success should never be the basis of a successful relationship. Let him live his script, and you live yours. Don't worry about how he will handle your success! The basis of a good marriage is very different.

Beyond all the success definitions that control our lives during these materialistically obsessed times, what a man wants from his wife is that she should be his greatest source of happiness. You be anything you want to be, but be the source of my happiness. What a woman wants from her man is that he should be her greatest source of protective love. You be anything you want to be, but be my fountain of love. And, as long as this need of 'happiness' of the man is addressed, and the need of 'protective love' of the woman is addressed, all other disturbances are mere details in a relationship.

If a man wants happiness in his marriage, then he has to give her lovely, loving and lovable times. If a woman wants love in her marriage, then she has to give him happy, happier and happiest times. ●

As long as this need of 'happiness' of the man is addressed, and the need of 'protective love' of the woman is addressed, all other disturbances are mere details in a relationship.

15

Is having sexual feelings towards my soulmate, whom I love and respect, and expressing them explicitly wrong? I am a religious person, and I am confused about this.

Soulmate has too broad a definition. To be interested in the body of those to whom you cannot rightfully gift motherhood or fatherhood, is not right. To feel with the body of the one to whom you will cause motherhood or fatherhood is rightfully right.

However, in a relationship that is rightfully yours, sex is a form of service. What you do for others, what they cannot do it unto themselves, is called service. Whether it is caring for a child, taking care of aged people, protecting the environment, because they cannot do it for themselves, you are doing it for them is service. Similarly, since sexual satisfaction is not something one can completely derive for themselves, providing them that fulfilment is actually a form of service.

Since you claim to be a religious person, let me clarify, when sex is not a mere seeking of the body but a culmination and expression of your deepest love for your beloved, because it enables you to forget yourself in the presence of the other, it gains a spiritual dimension. ●

What you do for others,
what they cannot do it
unto themselves,
is called service.

mahātria